Buenos Dias,

DIEGO!

The Bilingual Duck

TEACHING SPANISH EARLY

Starting with Preschool
by

VIOLA GRAYS-WILEY

Copyright

DEDICATION

This book is dedicated
to beginning readers
EVERWHERE,
especially Preschoolers through
First Grade Students- ESL
and Special Needs' students.
*An EXCELLENT RESOURCE for
Parents, Grandparents, and
Teachers!*

Buenos Dias,
DIEGO!
The Bilingual Duck

Good Morning,
James!

How are you doing?

Como estas?

Let's Count to 10!

0= cero   (Say-ro)

1= uno (Oo-no)

2= dos (doss)

3= tres (tress)

4= cuatro (KWA-tro)

5= cinco (seen-ko)

6= seis (SAISS)

7= siete ((SYE-te)

8= ocho (O-cho)

9= nueve (NWAI-be)

10= diez (DYESS)

<u>Now, our COLORS!</u>

English   *Spanish*

Yellow= amarillo

Red= roho

Blue = azul

White= blanco

Black= negro

Green= verde

Brown = marron

Orange= naranja

Purple= purpura

The sky is light blue! *English*
El cielo es celeste! *Espanol*

Are you hungry?

Tienes hambre?

Yes, I am hungry!

Si, tengo hambre!

No, I am not hungry!

No, No tengo hambre!

I want something to eat.

Quiero algo de comer.

I want some fish!

Quiero un poco de pescado!

On Sunday, I like to eat fruits!

El Domingo me gustas comer frutas!

On Monday, I like to eat hamburger with fries!

El Lunes me gusta comer hamburguesa con papas fritas!

On Tuesday, I like to eat
Tacos with cheese!

El Martes me gusta comer

tacos con queso!

On Thursday, I like to eat
vegetables with dips!

El Jueves, me gusta comer
verduras con salsa!

On Friday, I like to
eat pizza!

El Viernes, me gusta
comer pizza!

Do you like pizza?

Te gusta la pizza?

On Saturday, I like to eat

seafood!

**El Sabado me gusta
comer mariscos!**

Do you like seafood?

Te gusta el marisco?

I want to play outside!

Quiero jugar afuera!

Do you want to play
outside?

Quieres jugar afuera?

We can have so much fun!

Nosotros podemos divertirnos mucho? *(Masculine)*

Nosotras podemos divertirnos mucho? *(Feminine)*

Do you go to school online?

Vas a la escuela en linea!

I attend Duck Academy
online.

Asisto a La Academia de Pato en linea!

When the pandemic goes
away, I will go to Water
Academy.

Cuando termine la pandemia ire
A la Academia del Aqua.

All my friends will be there.

Todos mis amigos estaran

Alli! *(Masculine)*

Todos mis amigas estaran Alli! *(Feminine)*

I will see you later, my friend!

Hasta luego, Amigo!
(Masculine)

Hasta luego, Amiga!
(Feminine)

Good night!

Buenas Noches!

THE END